extreme threats

CLIMATE CHANGE

extreme threats

CLIMATE CHANGE

Don Nardo

MORGAN REYNOLDS
PUBLISHING
Greensboro, NC

Designed and produced by OTTN Publishing, Stockton, N.J.

Morgan Reynolds Publishing
620 South Elm Street, Suite 387
Greensboro, NC 27406
www.morganreynolds.com
1-800-535-1504

First printing

1 3 5 7 9 8 6 4 2

Library of Congress Cataloging-in-Publication Data

Nardo, Don, 1947-
  Climate change / by Don Nardo.
      p. cm. – (Extreme threats)
  Includes bibliographical references and index.
  ISBN 978-1-59935-119-3 (alk. paper)
  1. Climatic changes–Environmental aspects–Juvenile literature.
  2. Climatic extremes–Environmental aspects–Juvenile literature.
  I. Title.
   QC903.15.N37 2009
   551.6–dc22

                                    2009025704

extreme threats

ASTEROIDS AND COMETS   VOLCANOES
CLIMATE CHANGE   WILDFIRES

TABLE OF CONTENTS

In recent years, the rate at which the vast Arctic and Antarctic ice caps are melting has increased dramatically. This has raised international concerns about the effect that higher global temperatures, which many believe are caused by human activity, will have on the Earth's climate.

chapter one

Antarctica Shattered

The vast ice sheets covering the continent of Antarctica contain 70 percent of the world's fresh water. Scientists fear that if warmer temperatures melt the continent's ice sheets, rising sea levels will cause widespread flooding.

I n 2002, Earth's perpetually frozen continent–
Antarctica–was shaken by an event that some
scientists called shattering. For 12,000 years,
longer than humans have practiced agriculture, a
mighty ice shelf known as Larsen B had rested
along the continent's eastern edge. In Antarctica,
giant rivers of ice called glaciers slowly creep
toward the sea. When one of them reaches it, its
forward wall feeds an enormous floating mass of
frozen water–an ice shelf.

There had been signs of trouble in the region
of Larsen B for some time. In 1994, some cracks
had appeared in its surface. And in 1998, a small

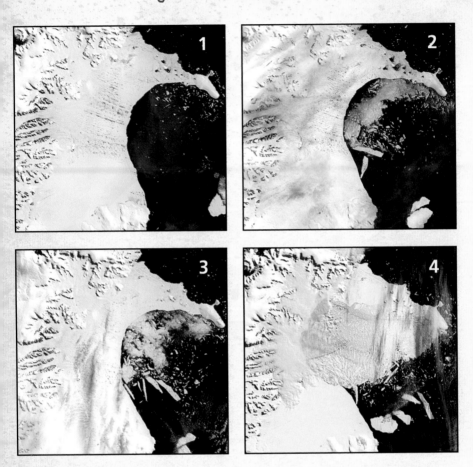

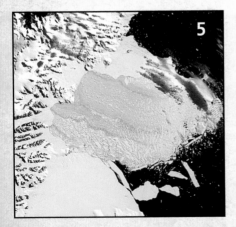

This sequence of satellite photos shows the collapse of the Larsen B ice shelf, a large floating ice mass on the eastern side of the Antarctic Peninsula, in 2002. The images were taken on January 31, February 17, February 23, March 5, March 7, and April 11 of that year.

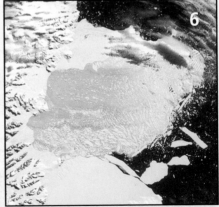

section of its outer edge had broken away. In addition, the nearby and much smaller ice shelf known as Larsen A had disintegrated in 1995.

Yet scientists felt there was no cause to worry about Larsen B. After all, it was nothing less than immense, with an area of 1,255 square miles (3,250 sq. km)–larger than the U.S. state of Rhode Island–a thickness of hundreds of feet, and an estimated weight of 500 billion tons. In the long ages of human history, ice sheets of that size had always remained stable.

In January 2002, however, what scientists thought was unimaginable happened before their astounded eyes. In only thirty-five days–a mere blink of an eye in geological time–Larsen B splintered and broke apart into thousands of pieces. Captured by ever-moving ocean currents, most of these icebergs steadily floated away, leaving behind a newly formed bay on the Antarctic coastline.

Unnatural Causes

The scientific world was abuzz over Larsen B's sudden demise. And though nearly all the experts were surprised by the event, some of them felt they knew what had caused it. Even before Larsen A's breakup in the 1990s, they had been studying Antarctica's weather and climate. Evidence showed that for long periods of time temperatures across most of that continent had remained stable. But then, in the second half of the twentieth century, unexpected changes had occurred. During those fifty years, temperatures on the peninsula adjoining the Larsen ice shelf had slowly warmed.

The increase in temperature had been small, but enough to lengthen the summer melt season slightly. And

Melt ponds and cracks can be seen at the left in this satellite photo of the Larsen B ice shelf, taken during the summer melt season in 2001. (In the Southern Hemisphere, where Antarctica is located, the seasons are opposite those of the Northern Hemisphere, so summer falls in December, January, and February.)

that had contributed to the steady demolition of the nearby ice shelves. During each subsequent summer, pools of melt-water had formed on these shelves. Before refreezing, some of the water had seeped down into cracks in the ice, in the process causing more melting and widening them. Eventually, the great masses of ice had become literally riddled with ever-widening cracks. And that had led to their ultimate doom.

One crucial question for scientists was why temperatures in that part of Antarctica had risen in recent years. The frozen continent is not only extremely cold, it also lies far from other large land masses and is not normally affected by their seasonal and more variable weather patterns.

Many scientists felt that the warming trend they had observed could be explained only by an abnormal and unnatural factor. There was already a name for it–global warming, although most experts have come to prefer the term climate change. (The general feeling is that global warming gives the mistaken impression that the entire planet is warming; whereas in actuality some parts of Earth are getting colder while others are growing warmer.)

Scientists had long known that Earth had undergone climate changes, both major and minor, many times in its long history. Until humans had arrived on the scene, though, these changes had had natural causes. Also, since the end of the last ice age, about 10,000 years ago, the planet had enjoyed a remarkably stable and constant over-all climate.

Only when humans began changing the makeup of the atmosphere through large-scale industrial processes in

Most scientists believe that human industrial activity over the past three centuries is causing global temperatures to change.

the 1700s, 1800s, and 1900s did this situation begin to change. Moreover, the amount of change has accelerated in the past few decades. Twenty of the hottest twenty-one years ever recorded happened between 1980 and 2005—2005 was the hottest of all, with record-breaking temperatures in many parts of the world. One dimension of this overall warming trend has been alterations in Antarctica's normally unchanging climate. "Really," says British climatologist John King, "we don't think there is much doubt that the collapse of the Larsen B shelf was caused by man-made climate change."

Europe's Killer Summer

Among the increasingly warm summers that occurred after 1980, for Europe the hottest occurred in 2003. Temperatures there soared into the 90s and low 100s F nearly every day and rarely dipped below 86 degrees F at night. A few days witnessed temperatures as high as 118 F. Overall, it was Europe's hottest summer in at least five centuries. Crop failures occurred all over the continent, and an abnormally high number of forest fires ravaged the region. Observers also recorded the lowest water levels ever in the Danube, Po, Rhine, and other major European rivers. Some 20,000 people died in Italy alone; another 15,000 perished in France. Many of the victims were elderly folks who had no air conditioning. Unable to escape their homes, they succumbed to dehydration and shortness of breath. Scientists and government officials in many countries fear that killer summers like this one may become more common in the near future.

Ice and Water on the Move

The possible consequences of major climate change are many and varied. But the case of the disintegration of the Larsen ice shelves provides a representative snapshot. At first glance, it might seem as if the only result of that event was the addition of few thousand extra icebergs to the southern sectors of the oceans. On a planetary scale, in and of itself that would not produce serious problems. After all, the Larsen ice was floating before the breakup; and its pieces were still floating (although some melted) afterward. So the event did not cause any rise in global sea levels.

However, the real threat lies in the glaciers that long ago created the Larsen shelves. Glaciers exist on land. If they were to enter the sea, ocean levels would rise, and many coastal cities across the world could flood. The problem is that the Larsen sheets had long acted as a sort of natural dam that kept several of the Antarctic glaciers in their place. As environmental writer Fred Pearce points out:

> The glaciers that once discharged their ice onto the Larsen B shelf are now flowing into the sea eight times faster than they did before the shelf collapsed. . . . And that faster discharge of ice from land into the ocean is raising sea levels. . . . The largest glaciers on the West Antarctic ice sheet [contain] enough ice to raise sea levels by six yards, [so] the stakes are rising.

Also affecting the possible stakes to humanity are numerous other melting glaciers across the globe. In the United States, Grinnell Glacier, in Glacier National Park in northern Montana, has retreated two-thirds of a mile (1.1 km) in the past fifty years and has almost disappeared. Many other U.S. glaciers have lost 20 to 40 percent of

These photos taken at Glacier Bay National Monument in Alaska provide a dramatic illustration of glacial retreat due to higher global temperatures over the past 70 years. (Top) This photo, taken in August 1941, shows the lower reaches of Muir Glacier; its tributary, Riggs Glacier, fills the valley, stretching to the ocean. (Bottom) By the time this photo was taken in August 2004, Muir Glacier had retreated out of view; it is now nearly five miles (eight km) to the northwest. Riggs Glacier has retreated as much as 2,000 feet (600 m) and thinned by more than 800 feet (245 m).

their volume since 1984. Even worse, the once massive ice sheet atop Mount Kilimanjaro, in eastern Africa, shrank by 82 percent between 1912 and 2000. It is expected to be totally gone by 2020.

In addition, the normally huge amounts of ice on the opposite side of Earth from Antarctica–the Arctic–are fast disappearing. The Arctic ice sheet had an average thickness of 11-12 feet (3.5 m) in the 1960s; by the 1980s it had been reduced to 8 feet (2.5 m); and in 2008 the ice was only about 3 feet (1 m) thick. The Arctic ice also covered a progressively smaller area during these same years. "This summer the ice pulled back even more, by an area nearly the size of Alaska" the *Washington Post* reported in October 2007:

> Where explorer Robert Peary just 102 years ago saw a great white disk stretching away apparently infinitely . . . there is often nothing now but open water. Glaciers race into the sea from the island of Greenland, beginning an inevitable rise in the oceans. Animals are on the move. Polar bears, kings of the Arctic, now search for ice on which to hunt and bear young.

Arctic sea ice has been decreasing at a rate of 9 percent per decade over the past forty years. The image on the left shows the minimum sea ice concentration in 1979; on the right is the minimum sea ice concentration in 2003.

Intolerable Consequences

These and many other examples of climate change have become known to both scientists and the public only in the last decade or so. The idea of a swift, dangerous rise in global temperatures is new and for many people hard to comprehend and accept. Until recently, many people, including some government officials, viewed the idea of climate change as overblown and alarmist. This was partly because they did not see major atmospheric temperature changes happening on a yearly basis. As late as 2004, former U.S. energy secretary James Schlesinger stated: "Satellite measurements over 24 years show no significant warming in the lower atmosphere, which is an essential part of the global warming theory." Even now to the casual eye it might seem that the planet's atmosphere is not warming enough to cause any serious problems.

However, scientists point out that Earth's average temperature is normally amazingly constant during a given

In 2007 the Intergovernmental Panel on Climate Change (IPCC), an organization of scientists supported by the United Nations, concluded that warming of the Earth's climate system is now "unequivocal," based on observations of increases in global average air and ocean temperatures, widespread melting of snow and ice, and rising global average sea level.

year and from year to year. And even seemingly small changes in overall global temperatures can have major consequences. Andrew Dessler and Edward A. Parson, authors of *The Science and Politics of Global Climate Change; A Guide to the Debate*, point out that "At the peak of the last

climate change a Hoax?

Many U.S. officials once scoffed at the idea that climate change, or global warming, was real. Furthermore, a number of them refused to accept that human activities could be a cause. Oklahoma senator James Inhofe (pictured at right), for example, said in July 2003:

> Anyone who pays even cursory [brief] attention to the issue understands that scientists vigorously disagree over whether human activities are responsible for global warming, or whether those activities will [cause] natural disasters. . . . The claim that global warming is caused by man-made [activities] is simply untrue and not based on sound science. . . . With all of the hysteria, all of the fear, all of the phony science, could it be that man-made global warming is the greatest hoax ever perpetrated on the American people? It sure sounds like it.

Even today, Inhofe and certain other high-profile American political leaders remain skeptical about climate change, despite a consensus among scientists that human activity is causing changes.

ice age 20,000 years ago, glaciers thousands of feet thick covered most of North America. [Yet] the average temperature of the Earth was only about 5 degrees C cooler than it is today. Thus, the prospect of a few degrees Celsius rise in global temperature over just 100 years . . . must be considered with the utmost seriousness."

Various alarming changes across the globe are sending signals that the world's climate is rapidly warming. One observer lists only a few of them:

> The world is now warmer than it has been at any point in the last two millennia [2,000 years]. And if current trends continue, by the end of the [twenty-first] century it will likely be hotter than at any point in the last two million years. . . . Nearly every major glacier in the world is shrinking [and] the oceans are becoming not just warmer but more acidic. The difference between daytime and nighttime temperatures is diminishing. Animals are shifting their ranges poleward. And plants are blooming days, and in some cases weeks, earlier than they used to.

What is more, these and other disconcerting effects of climate change are speeding up, says Harvard University energy and climate expert John P. Holdren. Indicating that these developments constitute a real threat to human civilization, he adds:

> Since 2001, there has been a torrent of new scientific evidence on the magnitude, human origins and growing impacts of the climatic changes that are under way. In overwhelming proportions, this evidence has been in the direction of showing faster change [and] more danger. [There is a] need for a massive effort to slow the pace of global climatic disruption before intolerable consequences become inevitable.

chapter two

Engines of Change

S cientists and many other people want to understand what is causing global climate change. In part this is because the steady warming of the planet is melting glaciers and raising sea levels to unwanted and even dangerous levels. During most of the twentieth century, the amount of this rise was relatively small—about .07 inches (1.8 mm) per year. But it rose to 0.1 inches (2.8 mm) per year between 1993 and 2003. Moreover, the U.S. Environmental Protection Agency (EPA) reports that sea levels along the U.S. east coast rose five to six inches more than the global average in recent years.

Too Much Water

Even more disquieting is the prospect that these figures may soon be obsolete. Scientists expect rises in sea levels to accelerate in the coming decades. The exact amount of rise is difficult to predict. But several experts say that if the world's glaciers continue to melt at increasing

A large chunk of ice breaks away from a glacier. The process by which icebergs are formed is called calving; warmer temperatures speed up this process. The diminishing Arctic icepack may lead to higher global temperatures, because polar ice reflects light from the sun back into space. As the icepack shrinks, less sunlight is reflected; instead, the sun's rays are absorbed into the oceans and land, raising the overall temperature—and fueling further melting.

rates, grim consequences will likely ensue. Several glaciers in Europe's Alps had lost the equivalent of 8 feet (2.5 m) of water by 2007. And at least eighty other major glaciers across the world have been losing the equivalent of 2 feet of water per year since 2000. According to Michael Zepp of the World Glacier Monitoring Service (MGMS): "2007 [was] the sixth year of this century in which the average ice loss of the reference glaciers has exceeded half a meter. This has resulted in a more than doubling of the melt rates of the 1980s and 1990s."

The biggest uncertainty, in the threat of rising sea levels, is the fate of the immense glaciers in Greenland and Antarctica. Greenland's ice sheets are steadily melting, and the melting rates appear to be speeding up. "Greenland is a different animal than we thought it was just a few years ago," says Penn State University scholar Richard Alley. "We are still thinking it might take centuries to go, but if things go wrong, it could be just decades. Everything points in one direction, and it's not a good direction." The problem is that the Greenland ice sheet is some 1,490 miles (2,400 km) long and more than 1.2 miles (2 km) thick, which adds up to many thousands of cubic miles of ice. If it all melted, sea levels would rise about 23 feet (7 m). Much worse would be the prospect of the Antarctic glaciers melting. Even if only a quarter of them broke down into water, global sea levels would rise about 49 feet (15 m).

The results of only a small fraction of such rises would be catastrophic for large numbers of people across the world. The inevitable effect would be changing shore lines on every continent and island. Many towns and cities that lie on coasts would be partially or completely flooded by only a 3-foot (1-m) rise in sea levels. As many as 600 million people (almost a tenth of the human race) live in low-lying river deltas and would be forced to abandon their homes. All islands lying within a few feet of sea level would disappear altogether. This would force their entire populations to relocate. The world has never seen, and would be hard-pressed to deal with, a refugee crisis of such gigantic scope.

Even if humanity is spared this dire scenario, a number of scientists predict, the consequences may still be harsh by normal standards. At the least, they say, major coastal flooding events would increase in both severity and frequency. Australian climatologist John Church, who is studying sea level rises, warns, "Coastal flooding events that today we expect only once every 100 years [such as the flooding of New Orleans by Hurricane Katrina in 2005] will happen several times a year by 2100."

Natural Forcings

The natural reaction to such gloomy, frightening forecasts is to call for efforts to stop, or at least to slow down, large-scale climate change. However, such efforts first require a solid comprehension of what is causing Earth to warm up. Scientists began to recognize, study, and understand the primary engines driving climate change only in recent decades. Though they have learned much, the global processes involved are extremely complex and still not fully understood.

Nevertheless, scientists have at least identified most of the basic processes that produce Earth's climate and cause it to change. The chief agents of change are what they call "forcings." A forcing is an ongoing event or series of

A U.S. Coast Guard fan boat cruises the flooded streets of New Orleans, looking for survivors after Hurricane Katrina submerged much of the city under more than six feet of water. Experts say that climate change will make devastating floods much more common in coastal areas.

events that change the energy or dynamics of a system. In this case, the system is the planetary climate. In past ages, before the number of people on the planet climbed in to the billions, all climatic forcings were natural. Large volcanic eruptions, for example, spewed dust and gases into the atmosphere, blocking sunlight and causing cooler climates for several years.

The sun itself, as well as Earth's movement around it, can also act as climatic forcings. According to the National

Climate vs. Weather

Many non-scientists tend to confuse climate and global climate change with weather and normal changes in weather in various regions. According to a 2008 explanation provided by the U.S. National Academies of Sciences:

Weather refers to hour-to-hour and day-to-day changes in temperature, cloudiness, precipitation and other meteorological conditions. Climate is commonly thought of as the average weather conditions at a given location over time. But it also includes more complicated statistics, such as the average daytime maximum temperature each month and the frequency of storms and droughts. Climate change refers to changes in these statistics over years, decades, and even centuries. . . . The accuracy of weather forecasts can be confirmed by observing the actual weather. Climate models, on the other hand, produce projections [predictions] many years into the future, making them difficult to verify.

Powerful volcanic eruptions pump tons of sulfurous ash into the atmosphere. When enough of these fine particles are forced into the air, they act as a filter that reduces the ability of sunlight to get through. Volcanic activity has caused changes in the Earth's climate in the ancient past; even some recent eruptions have been strong enought to effect global temperatures for a period of several years.

Academies of Sciences, "the sun's output is nearly constant, but small changes over an extended period of time can lead to climate changes. In addition, slow changes in the Earth's orbit affect how the sun's energy is distributed across the planet, giving rise to ice ages and other long-term climate fluctuations over many thousands of years."

A Giant Greenhouse

Neither the sun's output nor Earth's orbit have changed in the last few decades. So these natural forcings cannot have caused the recent warming trend. Scientists now recognize that an unnatural forcing–human activities–is the chief culprit. It started in a small way when people began to farm

Today, transportation-related combustion of gasoline and diesel fuel accounts for more than 30 percent of the carbon dioxide emitted in the United States annually. It is estimated that Americans operate more than 65 million cars and trucks. According to the U.S. Environmental Protection Agency (EPA), the typical passenger vehicle emits 5.5 metric tons of carbon dioxide each year.

and build cities, but its effects were insignificant until the height of the Industrial Revolution, in the 1800s and 1900s.

As factories multiplied across various parts of the world, huge amounts of smoke and various gases poured from smokestacks into the atmosphere. Later, emissions from cars and trucks added to the problem.

As early as 1906, Swedish chemist Svante Arrhenius suggested that these emissions might be turning Earth into a sort of giant greenhouse. Only a small number of scientists agreed at the time, mainly because very little evidence for it had yet been found. The notion that certain gases can cause air to get warmer or colder was not in question, however. Experts knew that excess amounts of water vapor, for instance, can warm up a given volume of air. This occurs because the water absorbs heat from sunlight.

A similar process occurs in a greenhouse. Sunlight passes through the structure's glass ceiling and walls and heats up the air inside. At the same time, the glass traps the warmth, keeping it from leaving the greenhouse. This causes the temperature inside to steadily increase. For this reason, the process in question became known as the "greenhouse

Other Causes of Climate Change Ruled Out

Human production of greenhouse gases is now believed to be the primary cause of climate change. The reason for this conclusion is that scientists have ruled out various natural forcings that have caused warming trends in past ages. These include changes in the sun's output of energy; slight variations in Earth's orbit; large-scale volcanic activity; and tectonic activity (the slow movement of giant crustal plates across the planet's surface). Two leading authorities on the issue, Andrew Dessler and Edward Parson, point out that orbital variations and tectonic activity "are simply too slow to cause significant warming over time periods as short as a century." Evidence indicates that the other forcings "are unlikely to have contributed more than a small fraction of the rapid warming of the past few decades. . . . since we know that human activities are responsible for recent increases in atmospheric concentrations of greenhouse gases over this time, this means that humans are responsible for most of the rapid warming of the past 50 years."

Chemicals called chlorofluorocarbons (CFCs) were once widely used in air conditioners and refrigeration systems. However, by the mid-1980s scientists recognized that CFCs contributed to the breakdown of a protective ozone layer in the Earth's upper atmosphere. The ozone layer prevents most of the Sun's harmful ultraviolet rays from reaching the Earth; without ozone, the UV rays would damage plants, kill tiny sea creatures called phytoplankton, on which larger fish depend for food, and increase the rate of skin cancers among humans. In 1987 most of the world's nations agreed to stop using CFCs; they were replaced with chemicals called hydrochlorofluorocarbons (HCFCs) and hydrofluorocarbons (HFCs). HCFCs and HFCs do not deplete the ozone layer; however, they are greenhouse gases, and scientists now believe that their use is speeding the pace of climate change.

effect." Also, the atmospheric gases that Arrhenius talked about became known as "greenhouse gases."

Besides water vapor, the chief greenhouse gases are carbon dioxide, methane, and ozone. Arrhenius proposed that as sunlight passes though the atmosphere some of it is absorbed by these and other greenhouse gases. On the positive side, he said, this process keeps Earth's surface warm and mild enough to support life. On the negative side, however, if the volume of greenhouse gases in the air increases too much, the planet could become uncomfortably warm.

Human-generated Greenhouse Gases

Today it is clear that Arrhenius was right. For more than two centuries, factories, cars, trucks, and other man-made sources have pumped huge amounts of greenhouse gases into the atmosphere. These gases have caused the air to warm considerably more than it would have through purely natural forcings. The result has been the initial stages of large-scale global climate change.

Scientists have determined that, besides water vapor, the most plentiful and potentially damaging of the greenhouse gases is carbon dioxide, or CO_2. Evidence shows that before the onset of the Industrial Revolution atmospheric levels of CO_2 measured about 280 parts per million (ppm). In other words, for every million molecules of air there were 280 molecules of CO_2. By comparison, in 2008 CO_2 levels measured about 385 ppm. More than half of the increase (55 ppm) took place between 1973 and 2008. The buildup of carbon dioxide in the atmosphere is clearly speeding up. Scientists believe that unless major efforts are made to reduce CO_2 emissions, atmospheric levels of the gas will reach at least 540 ppm by the year 2100. Some scientists worry that they could reach as high as 970 ppm.

Another potent greenhouse gas that is contributing to climate change is methane (CH_4). Methane is the main component of natural gas. It is generated by a number of large-scale natural processes, including volcanic eruptions and the rotting of vegetation. Another important source of methane is the gaseous wastes of humans and the cattle and other livestock they raise. "Like carbon dioxide, [methane] traps infrared radiation that would otherwise escape into space," Fred Pearce writes, adding:

> Indeed, molecule for molecule, it traps 25 times as much of the Sun's heat in the atmosphere as carbon dioxide. Hence the concern about the methane in the farts of cattle, whose world population has doubled in the past 40 years. There is roughly one head of cattle for every four human beings. Bacteria that break down cellulose in the guts of cattle convert between 3 and 10 per cent of the food that the cattle eat into methane. . . . Concentrations of methane in the air have been rising at 1 per cent per year, at least since 1950. This is four times the rate of increase of carbon dioxide. Levels are already more than double those recorded before the explosion in human activity on Earth that followed the Industrial Revolution. . . .Within 50 years, methane could be the prime greenhouse gas.

Through various industrial processes, people also generate other greenhouse gases, some of which do not exist at all in nature. Among others, they include nitrous oxide, sulfur hexaflouride, and CFCs (used in refrigeration systems). These gases exist in the air in much smaller concen-

As the human population grows, so does the amount of livestock needed to feed and clothe that population. Today, the U.S. Environmental Protection Agency estimates that cattle, sheep, goats, and other ruminant livestock produce about 80 million metric tons of methane each year. This is about 28 percent of global methane emissions from human-related activities.

trations than carbon dioxide and methane. However, some of them remain in the atmosphere longer. Molecules of methane have an average atmospheric lifetime of twelve years, for instance, whereas those of nitrous oxide remain in the air for 114 years, and those of sulfur hexaflouride for 3,200 years.

Whatever their individual concentrations and lifetimes, evidence shows that all the human-generated greenhouse gases combined are warming the planet. The result is significant increases in several ongoing threats to human civilization. These include not only melting glaciers and rising sea levels, but also droughts, water shortages, forest fires, and other potentially damaging events.

chapter Three

Too Little Water

The remains of a boat sit high and dry, showing where the water's edge was once located in this rapidly shrinking freshwater lake in Asia. If present climate trends continue, the Earth will become warmer and dryer, causing shortages of fresh water throughout the world.

A mong the various impacts that global climate change will have on humanity in the near future, a majority will occur in the middle latitudes. (These are vast the areas lying between the normally hot tropics and cold polar regions.) Included are the continental United States, the Middle East, most of Europe, and large parts of Asia, Africa, and South America. Scientists say this will happen partly because climate change is not affecting all parts of the world evenly. Instead, certain areas are and will continue to be affected more than others. Studies show that in particular, North America, Europe, and

parts of Asia will experience at least 40 percent more warming than the average global temperature increase.

The other reason this trend will seriously impact humanity is that a majority of the world's people live in these middle latitudes. Dessler, a professor in the Department of Atmospheric Sciences at Texas A&M University, and Parson, a professor at the Law School and School of Natural Resources and Environment at the University of Michigan, summarize some of the immediate effects on their lives:

> The combination of warmer summer temperature and increased humidity is likely to bring substantial increases in the summer heat index. (The heat index combines temperature and humidity to produce a measure of how hot it feels like.). . . [Some experts predict] an increase [in temperature] as large as 5-15 degrees C in July in the southeastern states of the USA. If you live there, you know how miserable that would be.

Life for millions of people will be more than merely uncomfortable, however. The ongoing and relentless decline of glaciers and mountain snowpacks around the world already has begun to reduce the amount of fresh water available for drinking, cooking, and irrigating crops. Computer climate models indicate that this trend will continue to worsen. The increasing scarceness of fresh water

Opposite: According to a 2007 report by the United Nations Environment Programme (UNEP), higher global temperatures could cause glaciers in the Himalayas and other mountain ranges of Asia to shrink by 40 to 80 percent by the year 2100. This would affect billions of people who depend on the Syr Darya, Amu Darya, Indus, Ganges, Brahmaputra, Yangtze, and Huang He (or Yellow) rivers for potable water, crop irrigation, and power generation.

will ravage large sections of the middle latitudes with droughts, deforestation (loss of forests), crop losses, large-scale fires, and much more.

Fighting Over Water?

The reduction in fresh water supplies is expected to become particularly dramatic in India, Pakistan, China, and other parts of southern and central Asia. For thousands of years the inhabitants of these lands have obtained most of their water from a complex network of rivers. Those rivers have long been fed by normal seasonal runoff from thousands of glaciers. (A majority of these large ice sheets are located in the Himalayan Mountains.) It is estimated that well over a billion people, perhaps a fifth of the world's population, are dependent on the water trapped in Asia's glaciers.

Because of the recent warming trend caused by climate change, these vital sources of water are shrinking at alarming rates. More than 460 Asian glaciers lost at least 20 percent of their volume between 1962 and 2001. Their accelerating melting rates threaten to deprive hundreds of millions of people of life-giving water. Some nations may also fight one another over that precious resource. "China and India already are water-stressed economies" involved in a "serious struggle for more water," one observer notes, adding:

> Water is getting tied to security in several parts of the world. The battles of yesterday were fought over land. Those of today are over energy. But the battles of tomorrow will be over water. And nowhere else does that prospect look real than Asia, the largest and most densely populated continent that awaits a future made hotter and drier by global warming. . . . With

the world's fastest-rising military expenditures, most-dangerous hot spots, and fiercest resource competition, Asia appears as the most likely flash-point for water wars.

Shortages of fresh water are also becoming more acute in the United States, as Stephan Faris, author of *Forecast: The Consequences of Climate Change, from the Amazon to the Arctic, from Darfur to Napa Valley*, reports:

> In the American West, disappearing snowpack combined with drought could lead to widespread shortages, especially during the summer months when demand is highest. The Colorado River could lose as much as a third of its flow in the next fifty years. One study gives even odds that by 2017 Lake Mead [straddling the states of Nevada and Arizona] could drop too low to provide power to Hoover Dam.

Intake valves rise above the water level at the Hoover Dam. As freshwater sources in the mountains have dried up, Lake Mead has grown smaller.

How Scientists Study Climate Change

Modern researchers use a wide array of methods to study climate changes in both the recent and distant past. One is direct measurements with thermometers and other instruments, an approach used for the past century and a half. Compiling eyewitness accounts of weather patterns and changes supplements such measurements. These accounts come from live interviews, accounts in modern newspapers and journals, and older historical records.

More indirect methods include drilling into ice sheets and the beds of oceans and lakes and removing samples. The samples, called "cores," contain valuable evidence for temperature changes, atmospheric content, and other information about climates in past eras. Dendrochronology, the study of tree rings, also aids in determining rainfall patterns and other climatic data.

Scientists also create and study complex computer models. These "simulate the behavior of the world's climatic system," noted scientist Brian Fagan explains. Such models use "increasingly large quantities of raw data derived from buoys, instruments records, [and] satellites. Computer models are used both to understand the natural variability of global climate and to measure the effects of different forcings."

Core samples taken from lakebeds and glaciers can be studied to provide data about how weather and climate have changed over centuries.

This reservoir in the mountains of southern England shows a significant drop in water level.

Worsening Droughts

Lake Mead is only one of many fresh water lakes that will shrink as a result of global climate change. This aspect of the warming planet is painfully highlighted by the fact that one of the world's biggest lakes is almost gone. In the 1960s, Lake Chad, in central Africa, was the sixth-largest lake, covering an area of 10,036 square miles (26,000 sq. km). But by 2000, it was only one-twentieth that size, at about 579 square miles (1,500 sq. km). Moreover, the lake's rate of retreat is speeding up, and it will likely be totally gone in a few decades. This trend is already a disaster for an estimated 20 million citizens of Nigeria, Cameroon, Niger, and Chad who depend on the lake for their fresh water.

Experts point to several reasons for Lake Chad's startlingly rapid shrinkage. First, the number of people using the lake for watering crops, drinking, and other uses multiplied rapidly in the twentieth century. But by far the largest factor in the lake's downfall has been a long series of severe droughts brought on by a steadily warming climate in the region. Scientists say that Lake Chad was more susceptible to large-scale evaporation than other large lakes because it was and remains unusually shallow. (It reached a maximum depth of only 34 feet, or 10 meters, in the 1960s.)

The worsening droughts in parts of Africa have their counterparts in the middle latitudes of several other continents, including North America. The droughts in the American West constitute one of the more troubling examples. As some of the western U.S. states continue to heat up in the next few decades, less and less fresh water will be available. Meanwhile, local populations are still expanding, and this is forcing towns and cities to desperately conserve their dwindling water supplies.

Raging Wildfires and Vanishing Forests

Another serious consequence of the water shortages caused by climate change is that entire forests and prairies are drying out. That makes them more susceptible to fires, as evidenced by both frequency and severity of wildfires across the world in recent years. Many U.S. states, particularly in the West, reported record numbers of forest and brush fires in 2006, 2007, and 2008.

These increasingly more severe fire years were not flukes, climate change experts say, but part of a larger

Trying to Keep Up With Population Growth

Robert Kunzig, author of the 2009 book *Fixing Climate*, comments on ongoing efforts to conserve supplies of fresh water in the American West:

> Every utility in the Southwest now preaches conservation and sustainability, sometimes very forcefully. Las Vegas has prohibited new front lawns, limited the size of back ones, and offers people two dollars a square foot to tear existing ones up and replace them with desert plants. Between 2002 and 2006, the Vegas metro area actually managed to reduce its total consumption of water by around 20 percent, even though its population had increased substantially. Albuquerque [New Mexico] too has cut its water use. But every water manager also knows that, as one puts it, "at some point, [human population] growth is going to catch up to you."

Cities in the western United States, such as Las Vegas, have to carefully monitor their water use to ensure that there is enough fresh water for their growing populations.

Cattle graze on a ranch recently cleared out of the Brazilian rainforest. Deforestation—the clearing of rainforest land, usually by burning—contributes to climate change, because burning trees and plants releases large amounts of carbon into the atmosphere.

trend of warming temperatures and drought. For example, there were six times as many forest fires in the United States between 1986 and 2007 than occurred in the same number of years before 1986. "Forests in the West are dying, most impressively by burning," Kunzig warns:

> The damage done by wildfires in the U.S., the vast majority of them in the West, has soared since the late 1980s. In 2006 nearly ten million acres were destroyed. . . . With temperatures in the region up four degrees F over the past 30 years, spring is coming sooner to the western mountains. The snowpack—already diminished by drought—melts earlier in the year, drying the land and giving the wildfire season a jump start. As hotter summers encroach on autumn, the fires are ending later as well.

No less ominous and distressing is the steady disappearance of huge expanses of rain forest across the world. Scientists point out that a mere 4 degree C rise in average global temperatures would be enough to change many rain forests into large swaths of scrub vegetation. Yet the effects of this warming trend are made worse by direct human intervention. The ongoing situation in Brazil's vast Amazon rain forest is an example. It is estimated that up to 12 percent of the Amazon forests may vanish from drought in the present century. But far more worrisome is that another 43 percent or more of the forests may be destroyed by Brazilian farmers and loggers. The farmers, who mostly remove the trees by burning, are adding enormous amounts of greenhouse gases to the atmosphere and thereby hastening climate change. Tens of billions of "tons of carbon are tied up in the leaves, branches, vines, trunks, and roots of the Amazon," one leading authority writes. "[This is] more than a decade's worth of the world's fossil fuel emissions. Every time the forest burns, some of that carbon is freed into the atmosphere. In Brazil, deforestation produces more emissions than all the cars and industries combined."

This sort of unchecked alteration of the composition of Earth's atmosphere is dangerous, many scientists caution. They say it is causing climate change to speed up, a trend that is partly evidenced by increasingly weird weather patterns across the globe.

chapter Four

Extreme Weather

One of the most interesting, at times perplexing, and ultimately disturbing aspects of global climate change is that it often affects different parts of the world in radically different ways. As the National Academies of Sciences explains:

> In some parts of the world, global warming could bring positive effects such as longer growing seasons and milder winters. Unfortunately, it is likely to bring harmful effects to a much higher percentage of the world's people. For example, people in coastal communities will likely experience increased flooding due to rising sea levels.

One major outcome of these very different climatic scenarios is what scientists call "extreme weather." They define it as alterations in temperature, rainfall and snowfall amounts, the intensity of hurricanes and other storms, and other weather phenomena that are more severe than normal. Experts often use temperature extremes as an example. A common misconception is that climate change will make the entire world warmer. This likely came about partly through the adoption of the frequently misunderstood term "global warming."

The reality is quite different. While some areas are getting hotter over time, others are experiencing longer and colder winters. Still others are learning to deal with seemingly abnormal swings back and forth between these extremes.

A Roller Coaster Ride

Because of global climate change, a bewilderingly diverse mix of extreme weather phenomenon can occur in various locales in a single span of a few months. Fred Pearce describes the roller coaster ride of wild weather that occurred in 1998, one of the warmest years of the last thousand years:

> The rain forests got no rain. Forest fires of unprecedented ferocity ripped through the tinder-dry jungles of Borneo and Brazil, Peru and Tanzania, Florida and Sardinia. New Guinea had the worst drought in a century, [while] East Africa saw the worst floods in half a century—during the dry season. [Meanwhile] Mongol tribesmen froze to death as Tibet had its worst snows in fifty years. Mudslides washed houses off cliffs [in] California. . . . The water level of the Panama Canal was so low that large ships couldn't make it through. Ice storms disabled power lines throughout New England and Quebec, leaving thousands without power or electric light for weeks, [but] unprecedented warm seas caused billions of the tiny algae that give coral their color to quit reefs across the Indian and Pacific Oceans, leaving behind the pale skeletons of dead coral.

Zeroing in on Tanzania, its many large-scale fires in 1998 occurred largely because of prolonged droughts.

These caused vegetation to be abnormally dry for long periods, making an upsurge in devastating fires much more likely. Tanzania used to have a fairly predictable cycle of droughts. A moderately severe dry spell took place about once every ten years. In the past two decades, however, droughts have occurred more frequently, and several have been more severe than average. The weather has become so extreme and unpredictable that farmers find it increasingly hard to plan ahead. One Tanzanian farmer, Julius Njame, complains:

> Water levels are decreasing every day [and] the rains come at the wrong time for farmers and it is leading to many problems. . . . We prepared our fields for planting seeds in the November rains. We waited but the first drop didn't fall till December 20. After a day, the rains stopped. Three weeks later, it started to rain again. But then it stopped again after a few days. Since then, we have had no rain.

Causes and Predictions

The precise causes of the extreme and unpredictable weather patterns that are occurring increasingly across the globe are still uncertain. But scientists do understand most of the main mechanisms involved. First, they say, our planet is tilted on its axis. That keeps sunlight from being distributed evenly across the continents and seas. Normally this alone does not lead to unusual weather shifts. But it does set up a situation in which some areas are naturally warmer than others at certain times of the year. When the added warmth produced by climate change is injected into this very uneven system, abnormal or even

Extreme rainfall can cause deadly mudslides, like this one that washed away homes in a mountainside village near Mexico City.

bizarre weather patterns can emerge. Washington State's Department of Ecology sums up this input of extra heat and gives some eye-opening examples of extreme weather that occurred in that state in a single year:

> CO_2 from cars, industries, and power plants traps heat near the Earth's surface. More heat means more energy. Adding so much energy to the atmosphere creates the potential for more extremes. Washington residents experienced [several such] weather extremes in the fall of 2006. First, record rains churned up rivers and caused landslides and floods around western Washington. Then, as the water began to clear, a record cold with ice and snowfall paralyzed parts of the west side of the state. That was closely followed by record gale force winds, 14 deaths, extensive property damage, and days of power outages for 1 million homes and businesses in Washington.

Washington and other states, as well as the federal government, have conducted a number of scientific studies of

Ice storms knock down trees and utility lines, leaving communities without electrical power.

climate change and its effects. One of the most comprehensive was the U.S. Government Climate Change Science Program, whose findings were released in 2009. All of these studies agree that bouts of extreme weather will become increasingly common in coming years. Along with several private-sector studies, they have made some predictions of what citizens of the United States can expect as a result.

Extremely hot days that once occurred every twenty years will happen every five years. And there will be both more and longer droughts in some parts of the country. Particularly in the West, severe droughts that used to occur every fifty years will happen every ten years. Also, the unusually dry conditions will lead to more forest fires and dust storms. What is more, there will be considerably less water available for city water supplies and crop irrigation.

Conversely, some non-drought areas will see more extreme rainfall events. Sudden heavy downpours will happen more frequently, especially in northern states. Freakish rainfall events that occurred every twenty years will happen every three years. In addition, the added water will make soils unstable in hilly areas, such as many coastal parts of southern California. The result will be more frequent destructive mudslides and landslides.

The Threat of Monster Storms

The largest of all extreme rainfall events, of course, are hurricanes. These giant storms spawned in Earth's oceans have occurred for millions of years and will continue in the future. The difference, researchers say, is that some future hurricanes will be much stronger and more danger-ous than those in the past. That this will happen as large

Some scientists believe that continued changes in the climate will cause the frequency and strength of tornadoes and other forms of extreme weather to increase. In 2008 and 2009, for example, the tornado season in North America began earlier than usual and lasted longer; many tornadoes formed in regions where they typically do not ocur. Higher global temperatures may have contributed to this, because warming alters the availability of moisture and influences air circulation patterns in the Earth's atmosphere.

Fear Grips the Insurance Industry

One troubling consequence of the threat of stronger hurricanes is a trend among large insurance companies to stop insuring property in hurricane-prone regions. In his book about climate change, *Forecast*, Stephan Faris reports:

> After Katrina [in 2005], insurers cut back on exposure [their risk of losing money] all along the coast. From the Texas docklands to the beaches of Cape Cod, coverage suddenly became much harder to find and much more expensive. Allstate, the nation's second-largest insurer of cars and homes, had suffered $5.7 billion in catastrophic losses in 2005. The company [said] it would not be renewing policies in Texas and Louisiana. [And] it would not be writing new coverage for homeowners in New Jersey, Connecticut, Delaware, New York City, or Long Island. "We believe what the scientists are telling us," a spokesman told Newsweek. . . . "We believe it would be bad business to continue to add to our risk." [Overall] the 2004 and 2005 seasons had set the insurance industry reeling, generating 5.6 million claims and insurance payments of $81 billion. By comparison, losses from hurricanes during the previous two years were $2.2 billion. . . . To those in the industry who had been sweating the impact of global warming, the twin seasons seemed to confirm their worst fears. As early as 1992, the [extremely wealthy] investor Warren Buffet had warned that "catastrophic insurers can't simply [base their present business practices on] past experience. If there is truly 'global warming," he wrote, "the odds would shift, since tiny changes in atmospheric conditions can produce momentous changes in weather patterns."

This radar image shows Hurricane Ivan striking the southern United States, while Hurricane Jeanne pounds the Caribbean nations of Haiti and the Dominican Republic, 2004. Scientists believe that as the climate changes, greater numbers of extremely strong hurricanes will occur each year.

sectors of the planet's surface grow warmer should not be too surprising. After all, hurricanes are essentially huge heat engines. They are born from and driven by warmth drawn from the oceans. The warmer the water such a storm encounters, the more energy it absorbs. That energy then manifests itself in stronger winds and the creation of bigger storm surges (walls of water pushed along by large ocean storms). As climate change steadily increases ocean temperatures, hurricanes will either become more frequent, stronger, or both.

The vast majority of scientists agree that this unfortunate scenario is already in its early stages. They cite a large body of evidence to support this view. The number of category 4 and 5 hurricanes worldwide each year has increased by

(Left) Hurricane Mitch caused this flooding and hurricane damage in Tegucigalpa, Honduras, in 1998. Mitch killed more than 9,000 people, making it one of the deadliest hurricanes in history.
(Opposite) Aerial view of flooded homes in Haiti caused by Hurricane Ike, 2008. This powerful storm killed 112 Americans and 74 Haitians, and caused more than $32 billion in damage to the United States, Cuba, Haiti, the Bahamas, and other Caribbean islands.

50 percent since 1970. (Hurricanes are ranked by the Saffir-Simpson scale. It has five categories, with the weakest hurricanes in category 1 and the strongest ones in category 5.)

Also, in 2005 so many tropical storms (the precursors of hurricanes) formed in the Atlantic Ocean that scientists ran out of names for them. That same year Hurricane Wilma became the most powerful Atlantic storm ever recorded. And another monster, Hurricane Katrina, slammed into Louisiana and Mississippi, killing more than 1,800 people and causing at least $100 billion in property damages.

Another disturbing sign of the growing threat of hurricanes occurred the year before. In March 2004 the first known hurricane ever to form in the southern Atlantic suddenly appeared. Dubbed Catarina, it struck Brazil, damaging or destroying more than 40,000 buildings. Even

more ominous was the fact that shortly before the storm's birth climatologists had predicted that the southern Atlantic would not begin to produce hurricanes until at least 2070. Now they fear that Catarina's formation may be a sign that climate change is escalating much faster than previously thought. If that is the case, some scientists worry that humanity may face something far bigger and more frightening than even the biggest hurricane—the onset of a new ice age.

chapter five

New Ice Ages

Aerial view of a glacier that stretches to the ocean along the coast of Greenland. Some scientists believe that warmer global temperatures could, paradoxically, create conditions that would lead to a new ice age.

At first glance, the idea that a major warming trend could lead to an ice age seems illogical, if not weird or even crazy. After all, the ice ages were periods in Earth's past when hefty portions of its surface were locked in a virtual deep freeze. Huge glaciers covered large parts of North America and Europe. The heavy ice sheets crept slowly across the continents, crushing forests, pulverizing hills, excavating new valleys, and giving birth to rivers big and small. Many animals and humans, then primitive hunter-gatherers, migrated southward. Some learned to live in the freezing margins of the glaciers. But for long periods of time the planet's comfortably habitable zones were limited to the tropical equatorial zones. That another such onset of giant ice sheets and bitter cold could result from today's rising global temperatures does appear to defy logic. Yet scientists have collected a considerable amount of evidence that shows it could actually happen.

The Great Ocean Conveyor Belt

Much of that evidence centers on what scientists informally call the ocean conveyor belt. (Its technical name is "meridional overturning circulation.") Because the Atlantic Ocean is the most critical component of this large-scale system, it is sometimes referred to as the Atlantic conveyor belt. It consists of a continuous circulation of ocean waters.

On the one hand, warm surface water in the tropics moves northward, gradually cooling as it goes. When it makes it to the northern Atlantic, the water, which is now quite cold, moves downward because cold water is denser than warm water and tends to sink. When this surge of water reaches the sea bottom, it starts moving southward under the ocean's upper layers. As it approaches the tropics, it grows warmer, which causes it to rise toward the surface once again. In this way, massive amounts of water constantly circulate through the seas. And the repeated introduction of warmer water into the otherwise freezing northern Atlantic helps to maintain a reasonably moderate climate across much of Europe, the northern United States, and Canada.

At least this is the way the great conveyor belt normally works. Scientists have found clear-cut evidence that now and then this enormous water circulation system temporarily shuts down. Among the chief reasons is a sudden influx of cold fresh water into the northern Atlantic. Fresh water is less dense than salt water. So when the fresh water enters the sea, it remains on the surface instead of sinking to the ocean floor. The cold fresh water now acts as a barrier that prevents the warmer tropical water from flowing in. As a result, the northern Atlantic stays cold all year. If the conveyer belt remains largely inactive for more than a few years, the climate in the adjoining land masses rapidly cools. And a minor ice age can ensue in the middle-to-northern latitudes.

Moreover, though temporary, such an event would not be short-term. According to Columbia University scientist Peter deMenocal:

> A shift in the ocean conveyer, once initiated, is essentially irreversible over a time period of many decades to centuries. It would permanently alter the climatic norms for some of the most densely populated and highly developed regions of the world.

Many experts say that the onset of colder weather patterns for many decades or several centuries would constitute nothing less than a minor ice age.

The Younger Dryas

Minor ice ages brought on by changes in the ocean conveyor belt are not just hypothetical. They have actually happened. In fact, two of them occurred on a small scale only a few centuries ago. Often referred to as the "little ice ages," the first spanned the period from about 1150 to 1460. It caused a major expansion of the glaciers on Greenland. And the freezing conditions it created compelled groups of Vikings who had recently built settlements there to return to Europe. The onset of the second little ice age lasted from about 1560 to 1850. This time glaciers in the Alps expanded, destroying many farms and villages in Switzerland, and causing New York City's entire harbor to freeze over in 1780.

The same kind of chilling event happened on a much larger scale several millennia earlier, at about the time that humans were first becoming civilized. Scientists call it the Younger Dryas. Roughly 15,000 years ago, after some

Nutrient-Rich Waters on the Move

The ocean conveyer belt not only affects global climate, but also sustains a large percentage of the life in the seas. According to a spokesman for National Geographic News:

> An estimated three-quarters of all marine life is maintained by a single ocean-circulation pattern in the Southern Hemisphere that pulls nutrient-rich waters from the deep ocean, brings them to the surface, and distributes them around the world. . . . The nutrient-rich waters help feed phytoplankton, single-celled plants at the bottom of the marine food chain that live at the ocean surface. As phytoplankton die, some slowly sink, decomposing along the way and carrying nutrients to the deep ocean. For years, scientists have wondered how these sinking nutrients, which seem lost to the deep sea, get back to the surface. [The circulation pattern of the ocean conveyor belt] provides an answer.

Ruins of a Viking church on Greenland. In the year 986, Vikings established settlements on Greenland; these thrived for centuries, but were eventually abandoned. Most scholars believe a "little ice age" that began in the twelfth century made it impossible for the Vikings to survive in Greenland. As glaciers expanded to cover the island, the ice covered grasslands that the the Viking settlers needed to pasture their livestock or grow food for themselves.

100,000 years of major ice-age conditions in North America and Europe, a warming trend set in. Glaciers retreated and plants reclaimed huge tracts of once-frozen wastelands. But in the midst of this period of moderation, about 12,800 years ago (ca. 10,800 B.C.), the Younger Dryas suddenly began.

The main cause was a natural catastrophe associated with an ancient lake. Called Lake Agassiz by modern researchers, it formed from the melting of large glaciers that had long covered what are now southern Canada and the northern United States. At its largest extent, the lake covered about 169,800 square miles (440,000 sq. km), an area larger than California. For reasons that are unclear, there was a major break on the lake's eastern flank. Most of its water rapidly drained through the Saint Lawrence River valley into the northern Atlantic. This sudden influx of cold fresh water into the ocean shut down the great conveyor belt. In the incredibly short span of a decade or two, ice-age conditions spread across North America and Europe.

The Younger Dryas lasted about 1,300 years. Exactly how humans adapted to its effects is unclear. They may well have taken a cue from their ancestors, who had made it though earlier ice ages partly by migrating southward to less harsh environments. Meanwhile, the advancing glaciers in Europe drew moisture away from the Middle East. As Fred Pearce speculates, this may have inspired new and ultimately important innovations:

> Some [experts] believe that dry conditions in the Middle East at the time [of the ice age] may have encouraged the first experiments with crop cultivations and the domestication of animals. And then the freeze ended, and temperatures returned to their former levels even faster than they had fallen.

This speedy thaw occurred because during the Younger Dryas glaciers once more built up in the Lake Agassiz region. This steadily removed cold water from the northern Atlantic, eventually allowing the conveyor belt to restart. In only a few years at most, the climate reversed itself. And about 11,500 years ago (9,500 B.C.), warmer weather patterns returned to the middle latitudes. The hospitable era that ensued is still ongoing.

Millions Threatened by Cold?

A number of scientists fear that our more climatically friendly era, which witnessed the rise of human civilization in its complex mixture of splendor and squalor, may soon end;

Indirect Ties to the Great Flood?

Another consequence of the climate change cycle triggered by the initial draining of Lake Agassiz occurred a few thousand years later and may have had an enormous impact on early human civilization. Evidence shows that as the climate turned colder during the Younger Dryas period, ice sheets built up again in the Agassiz region. But when the Younger Dryas ended, most of that ice melted and the lakebed partially refilled. About 8,000 years ago it drained again, this time causing a significant rise in sea levels. As the Mediterranean Sea rose, the added water broke through a natural earthen dam located at what is now the Bosporus Strait. This huge flood rapidly transformed a small fresh water lake on the other side of the dam into the Black Sea. An estimated 28,000 square miles (73,000 sq. km) of formerly dry land was flooded in only about thirty years and large numbers of people were forced to flee the region. According to University of Exeter scholar Chris Turney:

> People living in what is now southeast Europe must have felt as though the whole world had flooded. This could well have been the origin of the Noah's Ark story. Entire coastal communities must have been displaced, forcing people to migrate in their thousands.

Turney believes that climate change could have similar consequences in the near future:

> Rising sea levels can cause massive social change. 8,000 years [later], are we any better placed to deal with rising sea levels? The latest estimates suggest that by A.D. 2050, millions of people will be displaced each year by rising sea levels. For those people living in coastal communities, the omen isn't good.

(Above) The sun sets over ice floating in the Arctic Ocean. Scientists are worried that if the polar ice cap melts, the release of cold fresh water will affect the circulation of seawater currents, leading to colder temperatures. (Inset) A scientist with the National Oceanic and Atmospheric Administration (NOAA) drills through nearly four feet of Arctic Ocean ice to obtain cores; these will be used to examine past climate changes in the region.

and an ice age similar to, but perhaps not quite as severe as, the Younger Dryas may replace it. They speculate that melting glaciers in Greenland and elsewhere may provide an increasing flow of cold fresh water into the northern Atlantic. Once again, the ocean conveyer belt could slow to a halt.

But this time the victims would not be a few tens of thousands of nomadic hunter-gatherers, who could migrate southward with a minimal amount of effort. Rather, hundreds of millions of people living in modern towns and cities would be forced to adjust to a colder, harsher climate. At the same time, regions closer to the equator would grow warmer still and be subjected to drastic new rainfall patterns. In the words of NASA spokesman Edwin Schiele:

> Rising temperatures [may] melt the Greenland ice sheet. [Computer] models suggest that the resulting influx of fresh melt water into the polar sea could weaken the meridional overturning circulation, although not as drastically as the events thought to have triggered the Younger Dryas period. Still it could slow enough to reduce the flow of warm tropical water north into the polar seas. Temperatures over northwestern Europe could drop as much five degrees Celsius. [And] as less warm water flows north across the equator, the southern oceans will warm. The thermal equator (band of highest temperatures) would therefore likely shift south. The tropical rain belts would follow, altering rainfall patterns. Decreased downwelling [of ocean waters] would deliver less oxygen to the deep ocean, and decreased upwelling would carry fewer nutrients up from the bottom, potentially devastating ocean ecosystems.

Even if humanity manages to avoid a new ice age, experts say that global climate change will damage various natural ecosystems. In fact, this is already happening. And though humans will survive these changes, human health may be adversely affected in a number of ways. At the same time, many animal species will not survive the threats to planetary life that climate change increasingly poses.

chapter six

Threats to Life

Climate change threatens the future of many species. For example, polar bears and other Arctic and Antarctic creatures are endangered because their habitats are rapidly shrinking.

One of the factors that makes Earth unique in our solar system (so far as we know) is that this planet harbors life. Indeed, millions of species of plants and animals exist on Earth, all interwoven in a complex network of adjoining or overlapping ecosystems. (An ecosystem is a group of plants and animals that inhabit and interact within a given local environmental area or niche.)

Plant and animal species are extremely numerous and diverse. So it is hardly surprising that many of them, along with the ecosystems in which they live, already have been impacted by global climate change. As the National Academies of Sciences points out:

> Climate change is transforming ecosystems on an extraordinary scale, at an extraordinary pace. As each species responds to its changing environment, its interactions with the physical world and the organisms around it change too. This triggers a cascade [progression or chain] of impacts throughout the entire ecosystem. These impacts can include expansion of species into new areas, intermingling of formerly non-overlapping species, and even species extinctions.

Moreover, people are not physically immune to these impacts. Doctors and other experts already have recorded

The skyline of Shanghai, China, is barely visible due to the thick haze of air pollution, or smog, that hangs over the city. Increasing global temperatures will make such pollution worse, leading to health and respiratory problems among humans.

numerous health threats directly linked to climate change. What's more, a number of them are expected to worsen in the decades to come.

Increased Human Health Problems

Among the documented human health threats linked to climate change are various kinds of respiratory, or breathing-related, problems. Some of these are the result of polluted air in cities. In cities located in regions that are growing warmer, smog (a mixture of water vapor, smoke, and chemical pollutants) forms more easily and more often. Even moderate amounts of smog can cause breathing problems. And the ill effects are magnified for people who already suffer from respiratory ailments such as asthma. According to Paul R. Epstein of Harvard Medical School, an expert on the health effects associated with climate change:

> During the past two decades, the prevalence of asthma in the United States has quadrupled, in part because of climate-related factors. For Caribbean islanders, respiratory irritants come in dust clouds that emanate from Africa's expanding deserts and are then swept across the Atlantic by trade winds accelerated by the . . . warming oceans. Increased levels of plant pollen and soil fungi may also be involved. When ragweed is grown in conditions with twice the [normal] level of carbon dioxide, the stalks sprout 10 percent taller than controls but produce 60 percent more pollen. Elevated carbon dioxide levels also promote the growth and [spores] of some soil fungi, and diesel particles help to deliver these deep into our [lungs].

The spread of disease is another health problem connected to global climate change. Just as cold temperatures inhibit and slow the spread of most disease germs, the onset of warmer weather patterns tends to promote the multiplication of germs. This is particularly true in areas in which rainfall and humidity also increase. The World Health Organization (WHO) has confirmed that such areas are witnessing more cases of disease. Some regions also are reporting the introduction of diseases that did not exist in these areas in the past. One prominent example is Lyme disease, commonly spread by ticks. Large tracts of territory used to be too cold for ticks to thrive. But a number of such regions in the United States, Canada, Sweden, and other nations have experienced both the arrival of ticks and an upsurge in cases of Lyme disease.

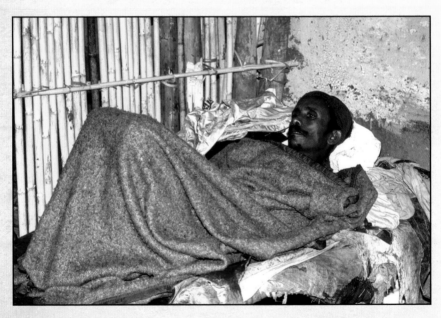

An Ethiopian man suffers from malaria, an infectious disease commonly found in tropical and subtropical regions. The World Health Organization (WHO) estimates that more than 300 million people around the world are infected with malaria each year, with one to three million dying from the disease annually. Warmer global tempearatures will increas the areas in which the *Anopheles* mosquito, which carries malaria, can live. This makes it likely that greater numbers of people will become infected in the future.

More worrisome is a rise in cases of debilitating mosquito-borne ailments. Among others, these include encephalitis, malaria, dengue fever, and West Nile virus. During most of the twentieth century there were no mosquitoes in Nairobi, the capital of the African nation of Kenya. But in recent years climate change caused increases in both temperature and rainfall in that city. As a result, mosquitoes began to breed there and malaria cases increased in frequency.

A similar situation existed with West Nile virus in the United States. That disease did not exist anywhere in the country until 1999, a year that witnessed much warmer, wetter weather patterns than normal. Once the West Nile microbes had achieved a foothold, they spread from the East Coast to the West Coast in only four years. "City-dwelling, bird-biting *Culex pipiens* mosquitoes thrive in shallow pools of foul water that remain in drains during droughts," Epstein explains.

> When dry springs yield to sweltering summers, viral development accelerates and, with it, the cycle of mosquito-to-bird transmission. During the hot, arid summer of 2002, West Nile virus traveled across the country, infecting 230 species of animals, including 138 species of birds, along the way. Many of the affected birds of prey normally help to rein in rodent populations that can spread [viruses and bacteria].

At Risk of Disappearing

Other living things besides people are threatened by climate change. For decades, biologists have noticed at first small but over time increasingly large alterations in animal behavior induced by warming temperatures. "Almost any-where you go in the world today," climate journalist Elizabeth Kolbert writes, "it is possible to observe biological changes [caused by warming trends]. A recent study of common frogs living near Ithaca, New York, for example, found that four out of six species were calling—which is to say, mating—at least ten days earlier than they used to, while at the Arnold Arboretum, in Boston, the date of first bloom for spring-flowering shrubs has advanced, on average, by eight days. In Costa Rica, birds like the keel-billed toucan, once confined to the low-lands, have started to nest on mountain tops."

In many cases, animals whose environments and ecosystems have been modified by climate change are able to adequately adjust. However, some species are facing changes that are too large and rapid to cope with properly. And these species are in danger of becoming extinct. Creatures that normally inhabit cold climates and that are experiencing significant warming trends are most at risk of disappearing forever. The most famous case is that of artic polar bears. Females of the species stop having babies when their weight drops below about 400 pounds. Robert Buchanan, president of the conservation group Polar Bears International, recalls:

> Twenty-three years ago when I first went up there [to the Arctic], you'd probably see one in seven mothers with three cubs. I haven't seen a mother with triplets in five years, and I'm up there a lot. Now what we're seeing is a female with two cubs. And the two cubs are very, very small because she's not able to feed them enough. She's not getting enough food herself.

The Threat to California's Wine Country

Plants are affected by climate change as much as humans and other animals are. According to the U.S. National Academies of Sciences, some recent changes in plants, including grape vines in California, have been beneficial. However, further warming brought on by climate change could reverse that trend:

> Wine is one of California's most important agricultural products. The industry [is] a critical part of the state's cultural fabric. . . . The quality of each [wine grape] crop depends on a subtle balance of climate, soils, and landforms. Climate changes during the second half of the 20th century generally improved conditions in California's premium wine regions as the incidence of frost decreased and the growing season began earlier. Further warming, however, would be unlikely to help wine growers in this area. One study concluded that if current greenhouse gas emissions continued, the projected warming would degrade the state's premium wine regions [and] that the area with the potential to produce premium wines could decrease by up to 81 percent.

Climate change could have a negative effect on California's wine production.

The primary reason that so many polar bears are eating less is that the effects of climate change are interfering with their hunting routines. These creatures are strong swimmers. However, they require a minimal amount of floating ice to hunt and eat properly. Because the arctic ice sheets are breaking up and disappearing at record rates, the bears must swim increasingly far to find the ice they need. Thousands of them have died in recent years. In May 2008 the U.S. Department of the Interior listed the polar bear as a threatened species under the Endangered Species Act. "Polar bears need ice," Buchanan emphasizes. "Without it, they can't hunt, they can't breed, and in most

Many Species Moving North

A number of animal species—including land and ocean varieties—are steadily moving northward in response to global climate change. Some are doing so because formerly colder regions are warming up and becoming more attractive as habitats. For example, the rufous hummingbird and Mexican green jay were long found only in tropical areas. Now they have moved into Texas and Alabama, where temperatures are growing milder. Similarly, Florida recently has witnessed the arrival of five species of tropical dragonfly. Other species are moving, or will move, northward to escape the warming trend. Young cod (a species of fish), for instance, need water temperatures lower than 46 degrees F to thrive and grow. As the waters off the eastern United States grow warmer, cod increasingly will be found in more northerly waters.

places they can't den. If you're not able to do those things, you won't have polar bears."

Some Species Crowding Out Others

Polar bears are not the only ice-dependent animals that are endangered because of climate change. Walruses are also having a hard time, as dwindling ice sheets make it more difficult to feed and nurse their young. In addition, large sectors of the arctic food chain are undergoing change so rapid that partial collapse is possible in some areas. In regions where for thousands of years there was only ice, snow and primitive lichens, warming temperatures have allowed small shrubs to begin spreading. These larger plants are crowding out the lichens. Because the lichens are the principal food of caribou (wild reindeer) in the winter, the caribou find it increasingly difficult to sustain themselves in the cold months. In turn, caribou are a crucial food source for large arctic predators like bears and wolves.

Many other plant and animal species in a wide range of global ecosystems potentially are endangered by climate change. Experts estimate that if present trends continue unabated, a mass extinction could occur. The consensus of leading scientists is that at least 20 percent of the planet's 1.7 million plant and animal species could go extinct in the next century. As awful as that figure sounds, though, it might actually be low. If a worst-case scenario occurs—in which the climate alters even more than expected—the extinction event could be even more markedly catastrophic.

chapter Seven

The Worst Case

There are presently thousands of scientists and other experts studying various aspects of climate change. Most of them have general ideas or educated guesses about how such change may affect the world and human societies in the next fifty years, one hundred years, and beyond. None of them can predict what will happen with any certainty, however. This is because thousands of individual factors, large and small, potentially can contribute to the nature and severity of climate change. And it is extremely difficult to know which factors will prove to be major, minor, or irrelevant in the years to come.

One such uncertain factor is human population growth. If the growth of global population slows or levels off over time, there will be less need for coal-burning plants, cars, and other energy sources that pump carbon dioxide into the atmosphere. This will help keep the levels of greenhouse gases in the air lower. However, if human populations grow markedly larger, much

View of the crowded city of Vijayawada, India, which is home to more than a million people. The world's population now exceeds 6.5 billion people and is growing at a rate of approximately 80 million per year. In the past, accommodating this natural growth has meant the destruction of wildlife areas to build new cities, as well as an increase in the consumption of fossil fuels to provide power. However, many climate scientists believe that such practices cannot be sustained in the future without affecting the climate.

more energy will be needed to support them; this may lead to a serious increase in the release of greenhouse gases.

Even if the planet's population does significantly increase, it is possible this could be counteracted by another factor. Namely, most countries, especially the most populous ones, could move away from energy technologies that are environmentally unfriendly. Massive research in and implementation of solar, wind, and other clean technologies might help minimize the adverse effects of climate change. The problem is that no one knows how many nations will adopt such an approach and to what degree. In addition, there are other factors that might affect the outcome of climate change but that cannot be foreseen. These include major wars, national economic collapses, global disease epidemics, large industrial accidents, natural disasters, and so forth.

Everyone hopes that when these present unknowns play out, the negative effects on humanity and the environment will be minor. But it is certainly possible that said effects will be major. "Our knowledge admits a fairly wide range of possible futures," Dessler and Parson point out, "which we can represent by a set of 'scenarios.'" With many different factors and possible futures involved, it is only natural to wonder what the outcomes of climate change would be in the worst case scenario.

Disappearing Rain forest and Feedback Loops

Scientists don't have to look far to find large-scale climate change disasters waiting to happen. They can look to the Amazon rain forest, in South America, by far the largest expanse of rain forest left in the world. Covering an incredible 2.1 million square miles (5.5 million sq. km), the Amazon is one of the planet's main climate engines. Each year it recycles vast amounts of heat and moisture that help to drive weather patterns across the tropics and far beyond.

The Amazon is also a gigantic reservoir of carbon. Its trees and other vegetation contain an estimated 77 billion tons of carbon and its soils about the same amount. As long as most of that carbon remains trapped in the forest, where it belongs, the Amazon's effects on climate change will be minimal. But in recent years a number of environmentalists have complained about Amazon deforestation. They point to Brazilian companies and settlers who are cutting down or burning many acres of rain forest each year.

A number of scientists say these losses are worrisome, to be sure. But they are even more concerned about droughts and forest fires that are fast increasing in number because of expanding global-scale climate change. The best estimate is that a given section of rain forest can withstand only two to three years of major drought. After that it will quickly dry out, die, and change into a desert-like expanse. When this happens, most of the carbon stored in its trees and soils will escape into the atmosphere in the form of carbon dioxide or methane. In turn, this will speed up climate change in the region. The destruction of forests will then accelerate, which itself will further feed the process. Some scientists think it is possible that half or more of the Amazon forest could disappear in this manner in the twenty-first century. This kind of event would be an immense catastrophe. It would drastically alter South America's climate while increasing planetary warming by at least 50 percent.

Opposite: South America's Amazon rain forest is the largest of the world's tropical rain forests; in 1970, it covered an area of about 1.6 million square miles (4.1 million sq. km). By 2009, more than 17 percent of the rain forest (270,000 sq. miles/ 700,000 sq. km) had been destroyed. Environmental scientists believe that rain forests must be protected to help mitigate the effects of climate change. Living trees remove carbon dioxide from the atmosphere, so shrinking forests reduce the planet's ability to eliminate this harmful greenhouse gas.

The process by which drought causes deforestation, which in turn creates more drought, and so forth, is not unique in nature. Scientists call such a process, in which the input and output of a system reinforce each other, "feedback" or a "feedback loop." Another feedback loop that could make climate change worse than expected involves water vapor. As various greenhouse gases warm the atmosphere, the evaporation of water naturally increases. Water vapor is itself a powerful greenhouse gas. So it, too, works to heat up the atmosphere, which in turn stimulates more evaporation. Still another feedback loop occurs when expanses of ice and snow grow smaller, as is happening today. Normally, ice and snow reflect sunlight back into space. So when they disappear, the sunlight strikes soil and/or plants. Because these absorb the warmth, atmospheric warming increases, which causes more ice and snow to melt. The problem is that the effects of feedback are difficult to measure in advance. So feedback loops could play a much larger role in future climate change than experts can presently calculate.

Nature's Doomsday Device

Even the potent effects of rain forest loss and feedback loops might, under the right conditions, be dwarfed by what has been called "nature's own doomsday device," which refers to a thick layer of permafrost covering large sections of Siberia, Sweden, Alaska, and other northern regions. Permafrost is soil, often mixed with peat (partially decayed vegetation), that remains frozen all year long. Huge expanses of permafrost have remained frozen since the beginning of the last major ice age. It is estimated that tens of billions of tons of carbon lie trapped in Siberia's permafrost alone; and hundreds of billions of tons likely exist in all the world's permafrost.

What worries many scientists is that for the first time in history large portions of permafrost are nearing water's melting point. If only a small percentage of the permafrost melted in the next decade or two, global climate change

Concerns About Methane

The issue of mass permafrost melting is further complicated by the fact that large amounts of methane may be released, as explained by observer Fred Pearce:

Unlike the tropical swamps of Borneo, which are degrading as they dry out, and producing carbon dioxide, the Siberian bogs will degrade in the wet as the permafrost melts. In fetid swamps and lakes devoid of oxygen, that will produce methane. Methane is a powerful and fast-acting greenhouse gas, potentially a hundred times more potent than carbon dioxide. Released quickly enough in such quantities, it would create an atmospheric tsunami [enormous wave], swamping the planet in warmth.

would markedly accelerate. And if all of the permafrost melted, it could by itself raise atmospheric temperatures by at least 5 degrees F. The combination of this increase with other ongoing effects of climate change would cause mass extinctions of plants and animals; kill or displace hundreds of millions of people; and make life miserable for the survivors. "It's like ready-use mix," says University of Alaska scientist Vladimir Romanovsky. "Just a little heat, and it will start cooking. I think it's just a time bomb, just waiting for a little warmer conditions."

Nightmare Situations

Still another aspect of climate change's worst case scenario is the prospect of the west Antarctic ice sheets melting. They contain "several million billion tons of water," Dessler and Parson point out. The flooding of coastal regions worldwide from such an event "would represent an unimaginable environmental and humanitarian catas-trophe. Most experts think these events are unlikely to happen in [the immediate future], but the risk of them happening much faster cannot be ignored."

If the west Antarctic ice sheets did melt in the space of only a few decades, one effect would be forced migrations of people living in coastal regions. The International Red Cross estimates that at least 250 million people will have to flee from coastal flooding. Another 50 million people, at minimum, will lose their homes to natural disasters, includ-ing strong hurricanes spawned in the warming oceans.

Even worse would be the melting of other large ice sheets in addition to those in Antarctica. The combined effects could raise sea levels by 65 feet (20 m) or more. In such a scenario, all of the low-lying nation of Bangladesh would be under water; so would the Florida Keys, up to a third of Florida, and the Nile River delta; and the streets of Sydney, Australia, New York City, Tokyo, Japan, and Bangkok, Thailand, would be flooded, forcing these megacities to be abandoned for good.

Having listed some of the situations that could or might happen, it should be emphasized that they need not occur.

A Giant Acid Bath

Still another nightmare situation that scientists fear global climate change is causing is a rise in the acidity of the planet's oceans. Since the advent of the Industrial Revolution, the oceans have absorbed an estimated 130 billion tons of carbon dioxide released by industry and other human activities. Some of the carbon dioxide has fallen to the seabed. But large amounts are still dissolved in the ocean waters. This has increased the production of carbonic acid, which is dangerous to creatures that require calcium carbonate for their shells or skeletons. Among these creatures are coral, starfish, sea urchins, shellfish, and others. Experts say that the acidity of the oceans could multiply three times by the end of the present century. The loss of coral reefs alone would be devastating because thousands of marine species dwell in them. Particularly vulnerable are pteropods, small sea snails that make up an important link in the ocean food chain. Growing acidity could wipe them out in a few decades, causing a partial collapse of the food chain, on which thousands of larger species, including humans, rely.

Some low-lying countries, such as Bangladesh, already experience severe flooding on an annual basis. As sea levels rise, this flooding will become worse, and may force millions of people from their homes as refugees.

A majority of scientists agree that humanity has the capacity to at least significantly slow the rate of climate change, and a number of nations are already taking initial steps to do so. The question is whether overall human commitment to this goal will be enough. As David Spratt and Philip Sutton, authors of *Climate Code Red: The Case for Emergency Action*, warn, "To make this commitment socially possible, we assume that nations will conclude that they need to go into emergency mode. But the type of emergency action needed is of an unprecedented form."

chapter eight

Fighting Back

U.N. Secretary-General Ban Ki-Moon speaks at the start of a 2008 United Nations conference on climate change. In recent years, the leaders of some countries have accepted that climate change poses a legitimate threat to humanity's future, and have begun discussing possible solutions.

Climate Change Conference

Poznań, Poland, 1 - 12 December 2008

I n the last decades of the twentieth century a fierce debate raged among scientists, government officials, and others over climate change. The principal points of argument were whether climate change is real, whether it is caused by human activities, and whether it poses a significant threat to humanity. There is now general agreement in the scientific community that the answer to each of these questions is yes and that the debate is over. Brian Fagan summarizes it this way:

> The scientific evidence documenting [human] contributions to a much warmer

world of the future is now beyond the stage of contro-versy. Now the discussions are changing focus, as we grapple with the long-term problems of reducing pol-lutants and living with the consequences of a world where ice sheets are melting and sea levels rising.

In other words, scientists, governments, and industries must stop arguing and apply themselves to counteracting climate change and minimizing its more harmful effects.

Pessimists vs. Optimists

Faced with this enormous task, some experts are gloomy about the future. They think it is already too late to signif-icantly slow the onset of large-scale climate change and its potentially disastrous effects. One such pessimist asks:

> Will we react [to climate change] by finally fashioning a global response? Or will we retreat into ever nar-rower and more destructive forms of self-interest? It may seem impossible to imagine that a technological-ly advanced society could choose, in essence, to destroy itself, but that is what we are now in the process of doing.

Other experts are more optimistic, however. They con-tend that there is still time to curb some of the worst effects of our steadily warming planet. They point to some past efforts in which coalitions of countries, industries, and sci-entists successfully reversed environmental damage by set-ting and achieving major goals. One of the most dramatic examples was the reduction of sulfur emissions and acid rain in the 1980s and 1990s. "When coal containing high levels of sulfur is burned," Dessler and Parson explain, "sulfur dioxide (SO_2) in the smoke makes the rain that falls

For many years, Al Gore has warned about the danger of climate change through books like *Earth in the Balance* (1992) and *The Assault on Reason* (2007). His award-winning documentary *An Inconvenient Truth* (2006) raised awareness about the severity of the climate crisis. In 2007, the former vice president and U.S. senator shared the Nobel Peace Prize with the Intergovernmental Panel on Climate Change, a scientific panel organized by the United Nations.

downwind of the smokestack acidic, harming lakes, soils, and forests. Over the past 20 years, a combination of advances in technologies to remove sulfur from smoke-stack gases, and well designed policies that give incentives to adopt these technologies, burn lower-sulfur coal, or switch to other fuels, have brought large reductions in sulfur emissions at a relatively small cost and with no reduction to electrical supply."

Numerous scientists, government officials, and concerned citizens hope that similar concerted efforts to slow and reduce the harmful effects of climate change will be equally successful.

Finding the Moral Courage to Act

Former U.S. vice president Al Gore has strongly advocated that national governments act quickly to reverse the effects of global climate change. Largely for these efforts he was awarded the Nobel Peace Prize in 2007. In his acceptance speech, delivered on December 10 of that year, Gore said:

> We, the human species, are confronting a planetary emergency—a threat to the survival of our civilization that is gathering ominous and destructive potential even as we gather here. But there is hopeful news as well: We have the ability to solve this crisis and avoid the worst—though not all—of its consequences, if we act boldly, decisively and quickly. . . . the Earth has a fever. And the fever is rising. The experts have told us it is not a passing affliction that will heal by itself. We asked for a second opinion. And a third. And a fourth. And the consistent conclusion, restated with increasing alarm, is that something basic is wrong. We are what is wrong, and we must make it right. . . . We must quickly mobilize our civilization with the urgency and resolve that has previously been seen only when nations mobilized for war. These prior struggles for survival were won when leaders found words at the 11th hour that released a mighty surge of courage, hope and readiness to sacrifice for a protracted and mortal challenge. . . . The future is knocking at our door right now. Make no mistake, the next generation will ask us one of two questions. Either they will ask: "What were you thinking; why didn't you act?" Or they will ask instead: "How did you find the moral courage to rise and successfully resolve a crisis that so many said was impossible to solve?"

International and Regional Efforts

The first such large-scale concerted effort to address global climate change was the Framework Convention on Climate Change (FCCC). Signed in June 1992, it was later ratified (formally accepted) by 190 nations, including the United States. Experts agree that the FCCC was no more than a basic starting point for dealing with the climate change threat. The parties involved promised to support climate-related research. They also pledged to do whatever they could to limit or reduce greenhouse gas emissions. But the treaty imposed no concrete or specific requirements or emissions levels to be met.

More specific goals and emissions levels were included in a tougher international treaty—the Kyoto Protocol, introduced in December 1997. It called on developed (highly industrialized) countries to reduce their greenhouse gas emissions by set amounts. The reasoning was that developed countries produce far more greenhouse gases than most developing (non-industrialized or semi-industrialized) ones. So the developed countries should bear most of the burden. European countries were required to reduce their emissions by 8 percent; the United States by 7 percent; and Japan and Canada by 6 percent each.

By early 2009, 183 nations had ratified the Kyoto Protocol. The United States was not one of them. This is partly because U.S. officials objected to the way the treaty classified developed versus developing countries. China and India possess large-scale industry and produce significant amounts of greenhouse gases. Yet, they were listed as developing countries, so they were not required to reduce their emissions, a situation the U.S. government viewed as unfair.

Some of the developed nations that ratified the Kyoto Protocol did decrease their production of greenhouse gases. Nevertheless, levels of these gases in Earth's atmosphere continue to rise. The reason is that China, India, the United States, and several other populous countries now release considerably more greenhouse gases than they did when the treaty was first proposed.

Meanwhile, other international and regional efforts to curb these substances are ongoing. The members of the European Union have pledged on their own to reduce

Diplomats from hundreds of countries hold a session during the December 1997 climate change conference in Kyoto, Japan. At the end of this conference, the Kyoto Protocol, an international treaty that sets limits on the emission of greenhouse gases by industrialized nations, was adopted. Kyoto's restrictions went into effect in 2005.

The member states of the European Union have taken numerous steps to curb greenhouse gas emissions. A banner promoting an EU campaign to raise public awareness about the issues, "You Control Climate Change," hangs from the Berlaymont building, the headquarters of the EU government in Brussels, Belgium.

their emissions by 20 percent by the year 2020. And in 2005 nine U.S. states (Maine, New Hampshire, Vermont, Connecticut, Massachusetts, New York, New Jersey, Delaware, and Maryland) formed the Regional Greenhouse Gas Initiative (RGGI). Its goal is to decrease emissions in these states by 10 percent, also by 2020. In addition, California hopes to lower its own emissions by 25 percent by the same year.

Cleaner Energy Sources

A major way that countries, states, and even many individual companies are trying to slow climate change is by using cleaner energy sources. This involves burning less coal, oil, and gasoline, which are prime culprits in greenhouse gas production. Wherever possible, the goal is to

In 2009, U.S. President Barack Obama promised to invest heavily in renewable energy technologies, setting a goal of doubling the amount of energy produced by alternative sources by 2012.

switch to alternative energy sources that create no harmful emissions. These include solar, wind, and geothermal power. Solar panels, for example, convert sunlight into electricity without any pollutants, emissions, or other harmful byproducts. Wind turbines and geothermal plants (which tap into heat generated deep inside Earth) do the same. Another reason these sources are so attractive is that they are practically inexhaustible, or renewable; they are often collectively called "renewables."

Experts point out that, despite their many advantages, renewables have certain disadvantages. First, they have low power densities. That means that they need to be applied on a large scale in order to produce even moderate amounts of energy. For instance, it would require many thousands of square miles of ground-level solar panels to meet U.S. electrical needs alone. Another drawback of renewables is that they provide energy on an intermittent basis. Wind turbines are useless on windless days, for instance; and solar panels do not work at night or on cloudy days. One way around the latter problem would be to place solar arrays in space to take advantage of sunlight twenty-four hours a day. But the cost of such technology is presently far too high. Another disadvantage of renewables is that in general they are extremely expensive.

Nuclear power plants are another possible alternative energy source. They, too, are expensive to build and operate. But they have a much higher power density than renewables and produce no greenhouse gases. A number of people object to such plants, partly because they worry about safety issues, including possible increased cancer rates from radioactivity. Another concern is the difficulty in disposing of dangerous nuclear wastes. Still another is the possibility of terrorists getting their hands on nuclear materials.

Nevertheless, a number of reputable scientists make the case that nuclear energy is one of the best ways humanity presently has of producing abundant energy without contributing to climate change. Renowned English scientist James Lovelock states:

> I am not recommending nuclear fission energy as the long-term panacea [solution] for our ailing planet or as the answer to all our problems. I see it as the only effective medicine we have now. [It will] keep the lights of civilization burning until clean and everlasting fusion, the energy that empowers the sun, and [cheaper, more effective production of] renewable energy [is] available. . . . We must conquer our fears and accept nuclear energy as the one safe and proven energy source that has minimal global consequences. It is now as reliable as any human engineering can be and has the best safety record of all large-scale energy sources.

With Ingenuity and Resolve

Most scientists agree that the choice between renewables and nuclear plants is largely a false one. They say that humanity will likely need both of these sources, along with several others, in order to prevent a potential climate catastrophe. Lovelock's reference to fusion power is telling. (Nuclear fusion works by forcing atoms together, releasing huge amounts of energy in the process; present nuclear plants utilize nuclear fission, which splits atoms apart, also releasing energy, though far less than fusion could create.) If and when scientists develop practical, affordable fusion technology, climate change, along with poverty, hunger, and many other age-old ills will no longer threaten humanity.

Until that time, however, the threat of climate change will remain real. To combat and overcome it, researchers, governments, and ordinary citizens alike will need to act

Nuclear energy offers a way to generate electrical power while reducing the emission of harmful greenhouse gases. The clouds billowing from this nuclear power plant are steam, rather than carbon-rich smoke.

with a combination of ingenuity and resolve. The question is not whether such an immense effort is doable. History certainly shows that people have the wit and grit to fight back when threatened. As Spratt and Sutton put it:

> When our society has responded effectively to great crises and threats in the past, it has put aside the partial measures and limited possibilities of "business as usual" and confronted enormous challenges, finding feasible solutions and pursuing them with single-minded determination. Our preparedness to do so again, when we are confronted with the greatest threat in human history, will determine our success or failure.

ca. 10,800-9,500 B.C.: As the ocean conveyer belt shuts down, the Younger Dryas, a small ice age, descends over large parts of the Northern Hemisphere.

ca. 10,000-9000 B.C.: Large-scale agriculture begins in the Middle East.

ca. A.D. 1150-1460: The Northern Hemisphere experiences another minor ice age.

1780: New York City's harbor completely freezes.

1906: Swedish chemist Svante Arrhenius warns that human industry might be causing a global greenhouse effect.

1912-2000: About 82 percent of the large glacier atop Africa's Mount Kilamanjaro melts.

1992: The first international effort to address climate change, the Framework Convention on Climate Change, is introduced.

1995: Antarctica's Larsen A ice shelf breaks up.

1997: Many countries sign the Kyoto Protocol, intended to reduce production of greenhouse gases.

1999: The West Nile virus first appears in the United States.

2000: Africa's Lake Chad has been reduced to only one-twentieth its size in the 1960s.

2002: Antarctica's Larsen B ice shelf breaks up in a little more than a month.

2002-2006: Faced with severe water shortages, Las Vegas reduces total water consumption by 20 percent.

2003: Tens of thousands of people die as Europe experiences its hottest summer in five centuries; U.S. senator James Inhofe calls climate change a hoax.

2004:   The first known hurricane to form in the southern Atlantic Ocean strikes Brazil.

2005:   The hottest year on record worldwide; Hurricane Katrina devastates the U.S. gulf coast.

2006:   Nearly ten million acres are destroyed by wildfires in the United States; Washington State experiences a barrage of extreme weather phenomena.

2007:   The United States experiences more wildfires than in any previous year.

2008:   The Arctic ice sheet shrinks to an average thickness of only 3 feet (1 m); the U.S. Department of the Interior lists the polar bear as a threatened species.

2009:   The U.S. government releases a study of climate change titled "The U.S. Government Climate Change Science Program."

Chapter 1: Antarctica Shattered

p. 14, "Really, we don't think . . ." Fred Pearce, *With Speed and Violence: Why Scientists Fear Tipping Points in Climate Change* (Boston: Beacon, 2007), 48.

p. 15, "The glaciers that once discharged . . ." Ibid., 48.

p. 17, "This summer the ice pulled back . . ." Doug Struck, "At the Poles, Melting Occurring at an Alarming Rate," *Washington Post*, October 22, 2007.

p. 18, "Satellite measurements over 24 years . . ." James Schlesinger, "Cold Facts on Global Warming," *Los Angeles Times*, January 22, 2004.

p. 19, "At the peak of the last ice age . . ." Andrew E. Dessler and Edward A. Parson, *The Science and Politics of Global Climate Change* (New York: Cambridge University Press, 2006), 3.

p. 19, "Anyone who pays even cursory attention . . ." Ibid., 10.

p. 20, "The world is now warmer. . ." Elizabeth Kolbert, *Field Notes from a Catastrophe: Man, Nature, and Climate Change* (New York: Bloomsbury, 2006), 12-13.

p. 20, "Since 2001, there has been a torrent . . ." Elizabeth Rosenthal and Andrew C. Revkin, "Science Panel Calls Global Warming Unequivocal," *New York Times Online*, http://www.nytimes.com/2007/02/03/science/earth/03climate.html?_r=2.

Chapter 2: Engines of Change

p. 23, "2007 [was] the sixth year . . ." *Science Daily*, "Glaciers Around the Globe Continue to Melt at High Rates," http://www.sciencedaily.com/releases/2009/01/090129090002.htm.

p. 23, "Greenland is a different animal . . ." Pearce, *With Speed and Violence*, 44-45.

p. 24, "Coastal flooding events . . ." Catherine Brahic, "Sea Level Rise Could Bust IPCC Estimate," http://www.newscientist.com/article/dn16732-sea-level-rise-could-bust-ipcc-estimate.html.

Sources

p. 26, "Weather refers to hour-to-hour . . ." National Academies Reports, 2008, "Understanding and Responding to Climate Change," 12, http://dels.nas.edu/dels/rpt_briefs/climate_change_2008_final.pdf.

p. 27, "The sun's output is nearly constant . . ." Ibid., 7.

p. 29, "are simply too slow . . ." Dessler and Parson, *The Science and Politics of Global Climate Change*, 73, 75.

p. 32, "Like carbon dioxide, [methane] traps . . ." Fred Pearce, "Methane: The Hidden Greenhouse Gas," *New Scientist*, http://www.newscientist.com/article/mg12216635.100-methane-the-hidden-greenhouse-gas-methane-from-cowsrubbish-tips-and-rice-fields-is-warming-the-earth-car-exhausts-may-helptheprocess-but-methane-from-the-arctic-tundra-could-be-most-damaging-of-all.htm.

Chapter 3: Too Little Water

p. 37, "The combination of warmer summer temperature . . ." Dessler and Parson, *The Science and Politics of Global Climate Change*, 83-84.

p. 38, "China and India already are water-stressed . . ." Brahma Chellaney, "Asia: Beware of Water Wars," http://www.risingtidenorthamerica.org/wordpress/2008/11/27/asia-beware-of-water-wars/.

p. 39, "In the American west . . ." Stephan Faris, *Forecast: The Consequences of Climate Change, from the Amazon to the Arctic* (New York: Henry Holt, 2008), 205-206.

p. 40, "stimulate the behavior . . ." Brian Fagan, *The Great Warming: Climate Change and the Rise and Fall of Civilizations* (New York: Bloomsbury, 2008), 10.

p. 43, "Every utility in the Southwest . . ." Robert Kunzig, "Drying of the West," *National Geographic*, 8, http://ngm.national geographic.com/2008/02/drying-west/kunzig-text/8.

p. 44, "Forests in the West are dying . . ." Ibid., 5, http://ngm.nationalgeographic.com/2008/02/drying-west/kunzig-text/5.

p. 45, "tons of carbon . . ." Faris, *Forecast*, 114.

Chapter 4: Extreme Weather

p. 46, "In some parts of the world . . ." National Academies Reports, "Understanding and Responding to Climate Change," 2.

p. 47, "The rain forests got no rain . . ." Pearce, *With Speed and Violence*, 19-20.

p. 48, "Water levels are decreasing every day . . ." John Vidal, "In the Land Where Life is On Hold," http://www.guardian.co.uk/climatechange/story/0,12374,1517935,00.html.

p. 49, "CO₂ from cars, industries, and power plants . . ." State of Washington Department of Ecology, "Extreme Weather," http://www.ecy.wa.gov/climatechange/extremeweather_more.htm.

p. 52, "After Katrina . . ." Faris, *Forecast*, 43-44.

Chapter 5: New Ice Ages

P. 59, "A shift in the ocean conveyor . . ." Pearce, *With Speed and Violence*, 147.

p. 60, "An estimated three-quarters . . ." John Roach, *National Geographic News*, "Ocean 'Conveyor Belt' Sustains Sea Life, Study Says," http://news.nationalgeographic.com/news/2004/06/0615_040614_SouthernOcean.html.

p. 62, "Some [experts] believe . . ." Pearce, *With Speed and Violence*, 150.

p. 63, "People living in what is now southeast Europe . . ." *Science Daily*, "Noah's Flood Kick-started European Farming?," http://www.sciencedaily.com/releases/2007/11/071118213213.htm.

p. 65, "Rising temperatures [may] melt . . ." Edwin Schiele, "Ocean Conveyer Belt Impact," NASA online, http://oceanmotion.org/html/impact/conveyor.htm.

Chapter 6: Threats to Life

p. 68, "Climate change is transforming ecosystems . . ." National Academies Reports, "Ecological Impacts of Climate Change," 2, http://dels.nas.edu/dels/rpt_briefs/ecological_impacts.pdf.

p. 69, "During the past two decades . . ." Paul R. Epstein, "Climate Change and Human Health," *New England Journal of Medicine*, October 6, 2005, http://content.nejm.org/cgi/content/full/353/14/1433.

p. 71, "City-dwelling, bird-biting *Culex pipiens* mosquitoes . . ." Ibid.

p. 72, "Almost anywhere you go . . ." Kolbert, *Field Notes from a Catastrophe*, 72-73.

p. 72, "Twenty-three years ago . . ." Faris, *Forecast*, 154.

p. 73, "Wine is one of California's most important . . ." National Academies Reports, "Ecological Impacts of Climate Change," 13.

p. 74, "Polar bears need ice . . ." Ibid.

Chapter 7: The Worst Case

p. 78, "Our knowledge admits . . ." Dessler and Parson, *The Science and Politics of Global Climate Change*, 77.

p. 82, "nature's own doomsday device," Pearce, *With Speed and Violence*, 77.

p. 82, "Unlike the tropical swamps of Borneo . . ." Pearce, *With Speed and Violence*, 78.

p. 83, "It's like ready-use mix . . ." Kolbert, *Field Notes from a Catastrophe*, 22.

p. 83, "several million billion tons of water . . ." Dessler and Parson, *The Science and Politics of Global Climate Change*, 87.

p. 85, "To make this commitment . . ." David Spratt and Philip Sutton, *Climate Code Red: The Case for Emergency Action* (Carlton North, Australia: Scribe, 2008), 177.

Chapter 8: Fighting Back

p. 87, "The scientific evidence . . ." Fagan, *The Great Warming*, xvii.

p. 88, "Will we react [to climate change] . . ." Kolbert, *Field Notes from a Catastrophe*, 187.

p. 88, "When coal containing high levels of sulfur . . ." Dessler and Parson, *The Science and Politics of Global Climate Change*, 2.

p. 90, "We, the human species . . ." Al Gore, Nobel Prize Acceptance Speech, December 10, 2007, http://nobelprize.org/nobel_prizes/peace/laureates/2007/gore-lecture_en.html.

p. 96, "I am not recommending . . ." James Lovelock, *The Revenge of Gaia: Earth's Climate in Crisis and the Fate of Humanity* (New York: Basic, 2006), 11.

p. 97, "When our society has responded . . ." Spratt and Sutton, *Climate Code Red: The Case for Emergency Action*, 177-178.

carbon dioxide (CO$_2$): A gas exhaled by animals, inhaled by plants, and produced by burning fossil fuels.

climate: Average weather conditions in a given region over time.

climate change: Global warming, extreme weather, and other climatic effects caused by human activity

climatologist: A scientist who studies climate-related phenomena.

computer model: A computer-generated simulation, or realistic imitation, of a natural or human-made process.

cores: samples for study taken from ice sheets, seabeds, and other natural formations.

deforestation: Destruction of forests.

dendrochronology: The study of tree rings.

drought: A prolonged lack of rainfall in a given region.

ecosystem: A group of plants and animals that inhabit and interact within a given environmental area.

feedback (or feedback loop): A process in which input and output within a given system form a loop and keep reinforcing each other.

forcing: An ongoing event or series of events that change the energy or dynamics of a system.

fossil fuels: Substances containing carbon that are commonly burned for energy, including oil, coal, and natural gas

geothermal power: Energy or power derived from heat produced deep inside Earth.

glacier: A large mass of ice that slowly expands and moves across the land.

global warming: Abnormal increases in the overall temperature of certain regions of Earth.

greenhouse effect: A warming effect that occurs when certain gases in Earth's atmosphere absorb heat and thereby make the air warmer.

greenhouse gases: Gaseous substances that cause the greenhouse effect, including water vapor, carbon dioxide, methane, and ozone.

ice age: A prolonged period of unusually cold weather in which glaciers and ice sheets expand.

ice shelf: A mass of ice that floats alongside an island or continent.

methane: A colorless gas released by decay of plant and animal matter.

ocean conveyer belt: A system within the Atlantic and other oceans that circulates warm and cold water, which affects the climate of the Northern Hemisphere

peat: Partially decayed vegetable matter.

permafrost: Soil that remains frozen all year long.

plate tectonics: The science that examines the slow movements of the continents across Earth's crust.

precipitation: Falling moisture, including rain, snow, drizzle, hail, and ice.

projection: A prediction.

solar power: Energy or power derived from the sun's light or heat.

weather: Hour-to-hour and day-to-day changes in temperature, cloudiness, and precipitation.

Dessler, Andrew E., and Edward A. Parson. *The Science and Politics of Global Climate Change.* New York: Cambridge University Press, 2006.

Fagan, Brian. *The Great Warming: Climate Change and the Rise and Fall of Civilizations.* New York: Bloomsbury, 2008.

Faris, Stephan. *Forecast: The Consequences of Climate Change, from the Amazon to the Arctic.* New York: Henry Holt, 2008.

Gore, Al. *An Inconvenient Truth: The Crisis of Global Warming.* New York: Viking, 2007.

Kolbert, Elizabeth. *Field Notes from a Catastrophe: Man, Nature, and Climate Change.* New York: Bloomsbury, 2006.

Lawson Nigel. *An Appeal to Reason: A Cool Look at Global Warming.* New York: Overlook Duckworth, 2008.

Lovelock, James. *The Revenge of Gaia: Earth's Climate in Crisis and the Fate of Humanity.* New York: Basic, 2006.

Mann, Michael E., and Lee R. Kump. *Dire Predictions: Understanding Global Warming.* London: DK Adult, 2008.

McCaffery, Paul, ed. *Global Climate Change.* Bronx, NY: H.W. Wilson, 2006.

Pearce, Fred. *With Speed and Violence: Why Scientists Fear Tipping Points in Climate Change.* Boston: Beacon, 2007.

Schmidt, Gavin et al. *Climate Change: Picturing the Science.* New York: Norton, 2009.

Spratt, David, and Philip Sutton. *Climate Code Red: The Case for Emergency Action.* Carlton North, Australia: Scribe, 2008.

Stern, Nicholas. *The Global Deal: Climate Change and the Creation of a New Era pf Progress and Prosperity.* New York: PublicAffairs, 2009.

Bibliography

Web sites

Numbers in **bold italics** refer to captions.